Contents

Foreword

This *Little Book of Big Bakes* is brought to life by the warm-hearted bakers of South Devon and by Rowcroft's Friends, Volunteer Ambassadors and staff. Each delicious recipe has been generously contributed to help raise funds for Rowcroft Hospice. By buying this book you too are helping the hospice to continue providing essential care for people in South Devon who are living with life-limiting illnesses. We are fortunate to be part of this giving community and we hope you enjoy making and sampling the cakes in this book.

Special thanks to Glenn Cosby, last man standing on the fourth series of the BBC Great British Bake Off. His exclusive recipe opens the book and his skill at judging bake off contests and encouraging Devonshire people to bake for charity is hugely appreciated by all of us.

Rowcroft Hospice provides care each year to more than 2200 people and their families across 300 square miles of South Devon; from Moretonhampstead on Dartmoor, to Dartmouth and Dawlish – more than 70% of our funding comes from the local community.

You can help us raise even more money to support people who need the specialist care that Rowcroft provides by joining our annual Rowcroft Big Bake campaign and hosting your own coffee morning, bake sale or bake-off contest.

Please contact us at any time if you would like to fundraise, donate or volunteer in any way to support Rowcroft. We'd be delighted to hear from you.

Thank you and happy baking!

Yours,

The Fundraising Team

raising funds for

Salted Caramel Cupcakes

For the cupcakes

200g caster sugar

200ml double cream

250g baking margarine
or salted butter

250g dark brown sugar

250g self-raising flour

4 large eggs

For the icing

150g salted butter

400g icing sugar

Makes approx. 20 cupcakes

Salted caramel

1   Melt 200g caster sugar over a medium heat into a light brown caramel – keep swirling the pan until all the sugar has melted.

2   Standing back slightly (it will sputter!) pour the 200ml double cream into the sugar.

3   Carefully stir over a low heat until the sauce is smooth.

4   Add two teaspoons of salt and leave to cool.

Cupcakes

5   Pre-heat the oven to 180°C, gas mark 4 and line your cake tray with paper cases.

6   Thoroughly beat the 250g margarine or butter with the 250g dark brown sugar. This is best done in a stand mixer or with an electric whisk; you want it to change completely in colour and be fluffy. This takes at least five minutes.

7   Add the four large eggs one by one to the mix while beating.

8   Add the 250g self-raising flour and combine. Stop mixing as soon as you can no longer see any lumps of flour, remember to scrape the bottom of the bowl.

9   Using a stand mixer or an electric hand whisk, combine the 150g salted butter and the salted caramel until it is completely smooth. Make sure the caramel is cool before you do this.

10   Fill the cake cases three-quarters full with the mixture and bake for 20 minutes or until a cocktail stick comes out clean.

Leave the cakes to cool in the pans for five minutes before transferring to a wire cooling rack.

11   Once the cakes are completely cool, use an apple corer or a teaspoon to scoop out a hazelnut-sized hole in the top of each cake; the bits that come out are chef's treats.

12   Take a teaspoon and fill each hole with some of the salted caramel – this may be a sticky job.

Salted caramel icing

13   Using a stand mixer or an electric hand whisk, combine the 150g salted butter and the remaining salted caramel until it is completely smooth. Make sure the caramel is cool before you do this.

14   Tablespoon by tablespoon add the 400g icing sugar until you have a firm, smooth icing.

15   Put a large star nozzle into a disposable piping bag and pipe a large swirl on each cupcake; start in the middle and work out and then come back into the middle.

Viennese Fingers

100g unsalted butter, softened

40g icing sugar

2 egg yolks

1½ tsp vanilla essence

125g plain flour

100g dark chocolate

30g unsalted butter

Makes approx. 20 fingers

1. Preheat the oven to 180°C, gas mark 4. Line two baking trays with baking paper.

2. Using electric beaters, cream the butter and icing sugar together until light and fluffy.

3. Gradually add the egg yolks and vanilla essence and beat thoroughly.

4. Sift in the flour. Using a flat bladed knife, mix until the mixture is just combined and smooth.

5. Spoon the mixture into a piping bag with or without a nozzle, and pipe into wavy 6cm lengths on to the prepared trays.

6. Bake the cookies for 12 minutes, or until golden brown. Allow to cool slightly on the trays, then transfer to a wire rack to cool completely.

7. Place the chocolate and extra butter in a small heatproof bowl. Half fill a saucepan with water and bring to the boil. Sit the bowl on the pan, making sure the bottom of the bowl doesn't touch the water. Stir occasionally until the chocolate and butter have melted together and the mixture is smooth.

8. Dip half of each cooled biscuit into the melted chocolate mixture and leave to set on greaseproof paper.

Tip

Store in an airtight container for up to two days.

Contributed by Claire's Cakes

Millionaire Shortbread

Shortbread

250g self-raising flour
75g butter
175g caster sugar

Filling

90g butter
90g light brown sugar
397g can of condensed milk

Topping

200g milk chocolate
50g white chocolate

Shortbread

1. Preheat oven to 160°C, gas mark 3.

2. Sift flour into a bowl.

3. Rub in butter until consistency of fine bread crumbs.

4. Stir in caster sugar.

5. Bring the mixture together to form a ball.

6. Roll out the dough to fit a 33 x 23cm loose-base tin and prick top.

7. Cook in the oven for approx. 20 minutes.

Caramel filling

8. Melt ingredients in a pan and bring to a simmer.

9. Simmer for five–ten minutes.

10. Pour mixture onto shortbread base and allow to cool.

Topping

11. Melt milk chocolate and pour over caramel.

12. Melt white chocolate and swirl on top of milk chocolate.

13. Leave to set and cut into fingers and serve.

Contributed by The Cake Stop

• Don't be fooled by the name, this fruit cake can be enjoyed at any time of year •

Cherry-Topped Christmas Cake

Cake

1145g mixed fruit

110g glacé cherries

120ml sherry or brandy

225g butter

195g muscovado sugar

1 tsp orange zest grated

1 tsp lemon zest grated

4 large eggs

2 tbsp marmalade

1 tsp almond extract

350g plain flour

2 tsp mixed spice

1 tsp ground cinnamon

1 pinch of salt

Topping

3 dessert spoons of apricot jam

Red, gold or green cherries

(gold cherries are available in most health food shops)

1   Place all of the fruit into a large bowl with the sherry or brandy, cover and leave overnight.

2   Preheat the oven to 150°C, gas mark 2.

3   Line a 24cm tin with baking parchment, also wrap double thickness brown paper around the outside of the tin, tie up with string.

4   Cream butter and sugar together, add the orange and lemon zest, beat in the eggs one at a time, then add the almond extract and marmalade, mix thoroughly.

5   Sift the dry ingredients together, then mix the fruit alternately with dry ingredients into the creamed mixture, make sure it is all combined well.

6   Put the cake mix into the tin, level the top and bake until a skewer comes out clean when inserted into its centre. This usually takes between two, and two hours and ten minutes, depending on your oven.

7   When the cake comes out from the oven, brush a couple of tablespoons of sherry/brandy over the top, and wrap the tin up in foil. When cold, remove the cake from the tin and re-wrap in foil, place in an airtight container.

8   You can 'feed' the cake on a weekly basis with your chosen liquor.

9   To decorate, melt the apricot jam, and brush over the top of the cake.

10 Cut the cherries in half and arrange in your chosen design.

Alternatively, decorate with the more traditional marzipan and royal icing.

Contributed by Terri Anthony, Rowcroft Volunteer Ambassador

Treacle Tart

170g white or brown bread
(crusts removed)
10g butter
2 large eggs
70ml cream
1.5g salt
720g golden syrup
Ready-made sweet
shortcrust pastry

1 Line a tart mould with the sweet shortcrust pastry and following the packet's instructions, bake blind. Allow to cool.

2 Preheat oven to 160°C, gas mark 3.

3 Blitz the bread to a fine crumb.

4 Melt butter until foaming and nut brown, strain.

5 Mix eggs, cream, salt.

6 Heat golden syrup and mix in butter.

7 Pour golden syrup mix into the egg mix.

8 Add breadcrumbs.

9 Pour into the tart mould.

10 Cook at 160°C until set, after approx. 25 minutes.

Contributed by Café ODE

Teddy's Chewy Flapjacks

150g butter (or margarine for
lactose intolerance or vegan)
125g demerara sugar
3 tbsp golden syrup
200g rolled oats
(check packet to ensure they are
gluten-free if required)

Makes approx. 12 flapjacks

1 Preheat oven to 160°C, gas mark 3.

2 Grease and line a baking tray 20 x 25.5cm.

3 Melt butter in a saucepan over a low heat, then stir in the sugar until fully combined.

4 Pour in the golden syrup and oats, then mix to ensure the oats are completely covered with the syrup mixture.

5 Pour the mixture into the tin and bake for approx. 30 minutes until golden brown.

6 Cool for five–ten minutes, then cut into the required number of servings.

7 Leave in the tin until completely cool before turning out.

Contributed by Teddy's Cakes

Irish Cream Liqueur and Chocolate Cheesecake

Biscuit base

500g chocolate digestive biscuits

200g butter

Filling

600g full-fat cheese

50g icing sugar

50ml Irish Cream Liqueur

284ml pot double cream

1 large pack Maltesers

Base

1 Butter and line a 23cm loose-bottom tin with baking parchment.

2 Place the biscuits in a plastic food bag and crush to crumbs using a rolling pin.

3 Transfer the crumbs to a bowl and add melted butter to the biscuit crumbs.

4 Mix thoroughly and place in the prepared tin. Chill in the fridge for an hour to set firmly.

Filling

5 Place cream cheese, icing sugar and Irish Cream Liqueur into a bowl and beat with an electric whisk until smooth.

6 Add the double cream and continue to beat the mix until it is quite firm.

7 Crush half the packet of Maltesers and stir into the mixture, reserving the rest for decoration.

8 Place the cream cheese mixture onto the biscuit base and leave to set for at least two hours.

9 Before serving, decorate with Maltesers and add extra Irish Cream Liqueur to taste.

Contributed by Carole's Cupcakes and Bakery

Macarons

Italian meringue

275g caster sugar
100ml water
95g egg whites
(approx. 3 egg whites)

Paste

275g ground almonds
275g icing sugar
95g egg whites
Approx 2g powdered
food colouring

Chocolate ganache filling

200g dark chocolate —
broken into pieces
200ml double cream

1   Preheat oven to 145°C, gas mark 2.

2   Blend the icing sugar and almonds in a food processor until fine. Sieve the mix into a large bowl and discard any large pieces left in the sieve.

3   In a small saucepan mix the sugar and water until there are no lumps. Bring to the boil over medium to high heat; do not stir. Place a sugar thermometer in the saucepan.

4   In a large metal bowl place 95g egg whites in readiness for when the sugar syrup reaches 120°C.

5   Once the sugar syrup has reached 114°C, start whisking the egg whites on a medium speed until they reach soft peaks. Once the syrup has reached 120°C, slowly pour the syrup down the side of the bowl, ensuring you don't splash yourself. Whisk on full speed for approx. five minutes. The Italian meringue is ready when it is glossy and forms stiff peaks; the side of the bowl will feel lukewarm, not hot.

6   Mix the remaining 95g of egg whites and food colouring into the almond, icing sugar mix to make a firm paste.

7   Once the Italian meringue is ready, it is combined with the paste in three stages.

NOTE: Ensure a nice, gentle mixing motion. If it is over-mixed, the mix will become too liquid and the macarons will become very flat when cooked.

8   Fold one third of the meringue into the paste. This can be mixed fairly vigorously to ensure there are no lumps.

9   The second third of the meringue must be folded in very gently, followed by the final third, again folded in extremely gently.

10   At this stage you may add the colourings of your choice.

11   The macaron mix is now ready to be piped. Holding the piping bag vertically, start in the middle of where you want your shell to be and pipe 3–4cm circles straight down onto non-stick baking mats, allowing a 2cm gap between each shell.

12   Bake immediately at 145°C, gas mark 2 for 17–19 minutes. Once cooked, allow to cool on a tray.

The macaron shells are now ready to be filled or frozen for use at a later date.

13   Make the chocolate ganache filling: warm the double cream and slowly stir in the chocolate pieces.

14   Do not boil the chocolate ganache or it will split and go grainy in texture.

15   Allow to cool slightly so it thickens before placing into a piping bag and filling the macarons.

Contributed by Ashburton Cookery School

Vanilla Cone Cupcakes

100g fat-free yoghurt
100g caster sugar
2 tsp vanilla paste
or vanilla essence
2 eggs
140g self raising flour
1 tsp baking powder
6–8 ice cream cones

Topping (stir together)

50g fat-free yoghurt
50g icing sugar
1 tsp vanilla

1 Preheat oven to 190°C, gas mark 5.

2 Stir together the yoghurt with the sugar and add one teaspoon of the vanilla paste or essence using a wooden spoon.

3 Gradually whisk in the two eggs.

4 Gradually add the flour and the one teaspoon baking powder and whisk the mixture again.

5 Add the other teaspoon of vanilla paste or essence and continue to whisk.

6 Divide the mixture between the ice cream cones on a baking tray.

7 Place in the oven and bake until risen and golden brown and springy, approx. 20–25 minutes.

8 Remove from oven and when cool, pipe a swirl of topping on the cakes to look like a delicious soft ice cream.

Contributed by Fun Kitchen Cookery School

Rocky Road

125g soft butter
300g dark chocolate (70% cocoa solids), broken into pieces
3 tbsp golden syrup
200g rich tea biscuits
100g mini marshmallows
2 tsp icing sugar for dusting

1   Melt the butter, chocolate and golden syrup in a saucepan.

2   Scoop out half a cup of the melted mixture and set aside.

3   Put the biscuits into a freezer bag and bash with a rolling pin. Aim for crumbs and some bits of biscuit.

4   Fold the crushed biscuits into the melted mixture in the saucepan and then mix in the marshmallows.

5   Tip into a baking tray about 24cm square.

6   Pour over the reserved melted mixture and smooth the top.

7   Refrigerate for at least two hours and then cut into squares.

8   Dust with icing.

Contributed by Louise Grant, Deputy Inpatient Unit Manager, Rowcroft Hospice

• These rich treats are traditionally served on Bonfire Night •

Yorkshire Parkin

340g self-raising flour
½ tsp salt
2 tsp ground ginger
1 heaped tsp bicarbonate of soda
120g oatmeal or rough oats
1 egg
½ pint of milk, warmed
170g margarine
170g sugar
170g golden syrup
170g black treacle

1 Preheat the oven to 170°C, gas mark 3.

2 Grease and line a baking tin 12 x 9 inches and about two inches deep.

3 Melt the margarine, sugar, syrup and treacle in a pan.

4 Warm the milk.

5 Beat the egg.

6 Mix the above ingredients with the flour, salt, ginger, bicarbonate of soda and oatmeal/oats and beaten egg.

7 Pour the batter into the greased and lined tin.

8 Cook in the preheated oven for one hour.

9 Remove from oven and cool on a rack.

10 Slice into squares when cold and enjoy.

Tip

Do not open the oven door during cooking.

Store in an airtight tin for 1–2 days to make the parkin sticky and even more scrummy.

Contributed by Elaine Moate for the Friends of Rowcroft

Bovey Biscuits

200g flour

120g desiccated coconut

150g oats

200g sugar

600g golden syrup

200g butter

1 egg

1 Preheat the oven to 180°C, gas mark 4.

2 Melt the golden syrup in a saucepan with 200g of butter and the egg.

3 Mix the flour, coconut, oats and sugar together in a bowl.

4 Add the syrup mixture to the dry ingredients and knead the dough until all the air bubbles are gone.

5 Roll out the dough on a floured surface and cut into rounds or other cookie shapes.

6 Bake in the preheated oven for 10 minutes or until golden brown.

Contributed by Bovey Castle

Raspberry and Coconut Slice

Base

100g soft butter
100g caster sugar
1 egg
210g self-raising flour
Raspberry jam
(or any other flavour)

Topping

100g caster sugar
2 eggs
160g desiccated coconut

1 Preheat oven to 180°C, gas mark 4.

2 Line an 8 x 8 inch baking tin with baking paper.

3 Blitz sugar and butter together until light and fluffy.

4 Scrape down sides and add the egg. Beat for one minute.

5 Scrape down sides and add flour. Mix well.

6 Press firmly into prepared tin; wetting your finger tips with water will prevent the mixture sticking to you.

7 Bake in oven for 15 minutes. Remove from oven to cool slightly, but leave the oven on.

8 To make the topping: mix the sugar with the eggs and coconut and stir together for two minutes.

9 Spread the jam on the base, then sprinkle on the coconut topping.

10 Bake in the oven for 20 minutes.

11 Allow to cool in the tin before slicing.

Contributed by Daisy Cakes

• A gluten-free cake that is moist and light •

Orange and Polenta Cake

For the cake

2 small oranges

5 large eggs

175g caster sugar

175g ground almonds

50g polenta (cornmeal)

5ml or 1 tsp baking powder

For the orange syrup

50g caster sugar

Juice of 1 large orange

1 Place the oranges, unpeeled, in a saucepan, cover with water and bring to the boil. Lower the heat, cover and simmer for 1¼ hours until very soft. Drain and cool for 30 minutes.

2 Preheat the oven to 190°C, gas mark 5.

3 Grease and lightly flour a 24cm spring-form cake tin and line the base with greaseproof paper.

4 Roughly chop the boiled oranges, removing any pips. Place in a food processor or blender and puree.

5 Whisk together the eggs and sugar for one–two minutes, then stir in the ground almonds, polenta and baking powder, followed by the puréed oranges.

6 Pour into the cake tin and bake for 40–45 minutes until light golden and just firm to the touch.

7 Leave to cool in the tin for ten minutes, then turn out and cool completely.

8 To make the syrup, place the sugar and 60ml (4 tbsp) water in a small pan and heat until the sugar dissolves. Boil, without stirring, until the syrup turns light golden.

9 Remove from the heat and add the orange juice. It will bubble and caramelise, so reheat gently until dissolved.

10 Serve the cake in thin slices with the warm or cold syrup poured over and crème fraîche.

11 Lightly dust with icing sugar.

Contributed by Lemon Jelli

• Serve as a dessert with cream, or enjoy simply with a cup of tea •

Chocolate Cake

Cake

450g softened butter
450g light brown sugar
8 egg yolks
340g dark chocolate
200ml warm water
400g sieved self-raising flour
8 whisked egg whites

Buttercream

60g softened butter
5 tsp icing sugar
1 tsp cocoa powder
Splash of warm water

Chocolate ganache

115ml whipping cream
170g dark chocolate
1 dessert spoon glucose

1 Preheat oven to 180°C, gas mark 4.

2 Cream the butter and light brown sugar together.

3 Add the egg yolks, melted dark chocolate and warm water and mix together slowly (it can splash out).

4 Fold in the sieved self-raising flour.

5 Then fold in the whisked egg whites.

6 Divide into two nine inch tins and bake for 55 minutes.

7 Remove from oven and allow to cool and turn out from the tins onto a rack.

8 Make the buttercream: whisk all the buttercream ingredients together until light and fluffy.

9 Spread the buttercream on the cakes and sandwich them together.

10 Make the ganache: warm the cream and glucose in the microwave (in short bursts to avoid boiling over), then all the chocolate and mix until all melted.

11 Allow the ganache mixture to cool slightly, then cover the cake.

12 Portion into 16 and garnish each slice.

Contributed by Cockington Chocolate Company

Swiss Tarts

250g flour
200g butter
60g sugar
½ tsp vanilla essence
Icing sugar to dust
Jam or lemon curd

1. Preheat the oven to 180°C, gas mark 4.

2. Line a muffin tin with paper cake cases.

3. Cream the butter, sugar and vanilla essence together.

4. Slowly beat in the flour.

5. Place mixture into a piping bag with a star tube in it and pipe into cake cases, leaving a small gap in the middle of each cake.

6. Bake in the preheated oven for approx. 15 minutes.

7. Remove from oven and allow to cool.

8. When cool, put a teaspoon of jam or lemon curd in the hole in the top and sprinkle the cakes with icing sugar.

Tip

Alternatively, you can pipe the mixture into rounds on a baking sheet and decorate with a cherry in the middle of each little cake.

Contributed by Startime Patisserie

Easter Cheesecake

200g dark chocolate
568ml double cream
360g cream cheese
120g icing sugar
200g mini Creme Eggs
450g chocolate digestive biscuits
200g butter

Cheesecake cream

1 Whip the double cream until stiff.

2 Sift the icing sugar into cream cheese and beat until smooth.

3 Add the cream cheese and icing sugar mix to cream and whip until combined.

4 Melt the dark chocolate in a bain marie and add to cream whilst gently mixing.

5 This process is best done using an electric mixer or food processor but if whipping by hand ensure all ingredients are fully combined and the finished cream is smooth and of an even colour.

6 Chop half the mini eggs and stir into the cheesecake cream, set the remainder aside for decoration. Refrigerate until biscuit base is complete.

Biscuit base

7 Crush biscuits into crumbs.

8 Melt the butter over a gentle heat then mix with biscuit crumbs.

9 Lightly grease an eight inch loose bottomed cake tin with butter and firmly press the crumb mixture into the base ensuring an even layer.

10 Bake the base for seven–ten minutes on 160°C. The base should still be soft and an even colour when taken out but will harden when cool.

Assembling the cake

11 When the biscuit base is cool spread the cheesecake cream over, ensuring a smooth finish. Refrigerate for at least three hours or overnight. To remove from tin, run a hot knife around the edge of the Cheesecake and release the tin. Use a palette knife to lift off the base and place on a serving dish.

12 Carefully slice the remaining Creme Eggs in half, use to decorate the top of the cheesecake by positioning in a circular pattern. Gently press the eggs into the cheesecake so that the top is level with the surface.

Contributed by Millie and Me

Mixed Berry Slice

Topping and base

225g oats

225g wholemeal flour

225g demerara sugar

175g butter

A pinch of salt

Filling

250g strawberries

250g raspberries

250g sultanas

90ml water

90g demerara sugar

Makes approx. 12 slices

1   Put all the filling ingredients into a saucepan and cook over a medium heat until the sugar has dissolved and the berries are soft. Be careful not to turn it into a jam. Set aside.

2   Preheat oven to 180°C, gas mark 4.

3   Line a baking pan approx. 26cm x 36cm with greaseproof paper.

4   Put half the topping base mixture into the pan and press down to make a firm, even base.

5   Add the berry mixture and distribute evenly.

6   Crumble the remaining topping mix over the top of the berry layer as if for a fruit crumble.

7   Place the pan in the preheated oven and cook for 45 minutes until golden brown.

8   Remove from oven and leave in pan to cool.

9   Cut into 12 slices.

Contributed by Seeds 2 Bakery

Seedy Peanut Breakfast Bars

125g butter

150g light brown soft sugar

125g crunchy peanut butter
(or other nut butter)

75g honey

Grated zest of two oranges

200g rolled porridge oats

75g chopped stoned dates

75g chopped apricots

50g sesame seeds

50g sunflower seeds

50g pumpkin seeds

Makes approx. 16 bars

1 Grease and line a 20cm square baking tin.

2 Pre-heat oven to 160°C, gas mark 3.

3 Over a low heat, melt together the butter, sugar, peanut butter, honey and/or orange zest in a large pan.

4 Add the oats, fruit and two thirds of the seeds. Mix together until well combined.

5 Pour the mixture in the baking tray and smooth the surface.

6 Sprinkle the remaining seeds on top.

7 Place in the preheated oven and bake for around 30 minutes, until golden brown on top.

8 Remove from the oven and allow to cool in the tin.

9 Once completely cold, turn out and cut into bars.

Tip

These delicious breakfast bars keep for five days in a tin.

Contributed by Café Alf Resco

Lemon Zest Cake

Cake

400g margarine

400g caster sugar

400g self raising flour

8 medium eggs

2 tsp vanilla extract (not essence)

Zest of 4 lemons

Lemon sugar syrup

60ml lemon juice

60g caster sugar

15ml limoncello (optional)

Buttercream filling and outer coating

500g salted butter

1kg sifted icing sugar

1 tbsp soft cream cheese

2 tsp vanilla extract

4 tbsp lemon curd

4 tsp limoncello (optional)

Lemon curd for filling

1 Preheat the oven to 160°C, gas mark 3. Prepare two eight inch sandwich cake tins — grease the sides and line the bottom with baking paper.

2 Beat the margarine and sugar together until light and fluffy.

3 Add the eggs one at a time, beating well after each addition.

4 Sift in the flour and mix thoroughly.

5 Add the vanilla extract and the lemon zest.

6 Pour the mixture into the cake tins.

7 Place into the oven and bake for 30–40 minutes until the cakes have risen, are lightly golden and an inserted skewer comes out clean.

8 Once out of the oven, let the cake rest in the tin for five minutes then turn out onto a wire rack to cool.

9 Whilst still warm brush some of the lemon syrup onto the top and bottom of both cakes. Reserve some of the syrup for later.

Syrup

10 Place the sugar and lemon juice in a saucepan.

11 Heat until all the sugar has dissolved. Allow to cool and then add the Limoncello.

Buttercream

12 Cream the butter until it has become a lighter colour (approx. ten minutes).

13 Sift the icing sugar into the bowl and mix thoroughly with the butter.

14 Add the cream cheese, vanilla essence and limoncello and mix thoroughly.

Recipe continued ▶

Contributed by Daisy, Molly and Me

Lemon Zest Cake continued

15 Add the lemon curd and mix.

Levelling and Filling

16 Trim the dome from the top of both cakes using a sharp knife to make a flat surface.

17 Cut each cake in half horizontally. This will give you four layers.

18 Place the bottom layer of one cake on a cake board or flat plate.

19 Brush some of the lemon syrup across it to keep it moist.

20 Spread with a generous layer of buttercream.

21 Place the next layer on top and repeat step 20.

22 Spread with a very thin layer of buttercream and then with a layer of lemon curd. The thin layer of buttercream helps prevent the lemon curd from soaking into the cake.

23 Place the top of the other cake on top of these two tiers.

24 Repeat steps 20 and 21.

25 Place the last layer on top making sure you have turned it over so the bottom is uppermost.

26 Check the cake is flat before putting it in the fridge for about 30 minutes to allow the buttercream to set a little.

27 Take the cake out of the fridge and spread buttercream liberally round the sides.

28 Using a straight knife or side scraper remove the excess buttercream and smooth the sides. Make sure the knife or scraper is held straight to ensure the sides are vertical.

29 Spread a liberal amount of buttercream on the top of the cake and use a long flat knife or scraper to pull across the top to smooth the surface.

30 Put the cake in the fridge for approx. 30 minutes to allow the buttercream to set.

31 If you want to decorate the cake, use a suitable star nozzle and piping bag filled with buttercream to pipe swirls round the bottom and top edge or use cutters to create sugar flowers etc.

Tip

To get more portions from a round cake, always cut in a grid rather than wedges.

Contributed by Daisy, Molly and Me